Make and Eat

Biscuits
and Cakes

Susannah Blake

WAYLAND

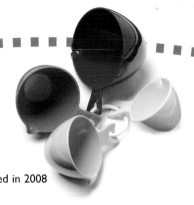

First published in 2008
by Wayland

This edition reprinted by Wayland in 2008

Copyright © Wayland 2008

Wayland
338 Euston Road
London NW1 3BH

Wayland
Level 17/207 Kent Street
Sydney NSW 2000

Senior editor: Jennifer Schofield
Designer: Jane Hawkins
Photographer: Andy Crawford
Proofreader: Susie Brooks

The author and publisher would like to thank the following
models: Adam Menditta, Harriet Couch, Demi Mensah, Robert
Kilminster, Aneesa Qureshi, Kaine Zachary Levy, Emel Augustin,
Claire Shanahan.

All photographs by Andy Crawford except page 4: Kevin
Fleming/Corbis; page 5 Marie Dubrac/ANYONE/Getty images

CIP data
  Blake, Susannah
  Biscuits & cakes. - (Make & eat)
  1. Biscuits - Juvenile literature 2. Cake - Juvenile
  literature 3. Baking - Juvenile literature
  I. Title
  641.8'15

ISBN: 978 0 7502 5356 7

Printed in China

Wayland is a division of Hachette Children's Books,
an Hachette Livre UK company.
www.hachettelivre.co.uk

Note to parents and teachers:

The recipes in this book are intended
to be made by children. However, we
recommend adult supervision at all times,
especially when using kitchen equipment,
as the Publisher cannot be held
responsible for any injury.

Contents

All about biscuits and cakes

There are many kinds of biscuit and cake. They can have different tastes, textures, colours and shapes depending on the ingredients used. Often they are sweet, but they can be savoury, too. Most biscuits and cakes are baked in the oven, but some do not need baking and are chilled in the fridge instead.

DIFFERENT KINDS OF BISCUIT AND CAKE

Butter, sugar, eggs and flour are the main ingredients used to make biscuits and cakes. But you can add other ingredients such as oats, syrup, dried fruit, chocolate and nuts. The way you combine and cook these ingredients can give miraculous results. Different combinations will produce different kinds of biscuit and cake. Some will be soft and chewy, some will be crisp and crumbly, while others will be light and airy.

BAKING TINS AND SHEETS

Cakes and biscuits are usually baked in some kind of tin or case. For example, little cupcake cases can be used to make fairy cakes (see right) or if you are making a large cake, you would use sandwich cake tins, which are perfect for stacking one cake on top of another. Biscuits and cookies are often cooked on baking sheets – these are metal trays that can go in the oven.

DIFFERENT DECORATIONS

Most biscuits and cakes can be served plain – but they can be decorated, too. This not only looks pretty and tastes good, but it can also be great fun! You can decorate cakes and cookies before baking. Try sprinkling flaked nuts or coarse sugar on top of cakes or soft cookie mixtures. Alternatively, you can press on whole nuts or glacé fruits.

Some people prefer to decorate cakes and cookies once they have been baked. Simple glacé icing or butter icing are easy to make (see page 12–13) and can be spooned or spread on top of a cooked cake or biscuit. If you like, you can add more decorations. Pretty coloured sweets, hundreds and thousands or fruit and nuts all look good. You could also add a dusting of icing sugar to cakes.

GET STARTED!

In this book you can learn to make all kinds of biscuit and cake. All the recipes use everyday kitchen equipment, such as knives, spoons, forks and chopping boards. You can see pictures of the different equipment that you may need on page 23. Before you start, check that you have all the equipment that you will need and make a list of any ingredients you need to buy. Check too that there is an adult to help you, especially with the recipes that involve using the cooker or oven.

When you have everything you need, make sure all the kitchen surfaces are clean and wash your hands well with soap and water. If you have long hair, tie it back. Always wash raw fruits and vegetables under cold running water before preparing or cooking them. Then, put on an apron and get baking!

Fruity flapjacks

These chewy flapjacks make a great treat to pop into your lunchbox. The flapjacks will look soft when you take them out of the oven, but they firm up when they cool.

INGREDIENTS
For 16 flapjacks:
- 125g butter, plus extra for greasing
- 75g ready-to-eat dried apricots
- 125g demerara sugar
- 5 tbsp golden syrup
- 200g rolled oats
- 2 tbsp sunflower seeds
- 2 tbsp pumpkin seeds

EXTRA EQUIPMENT
20cm x 20cm cake tin
Ask an adult to help you use the cooker and oven.

1 Preheat the oven to 180°C/350°F/Gas 4. Grease the cake tin with butter, making sure the base and sides are coated all over.

ROLLED OATS

Oats are a type of cereal that grow well in moist, cool climates. The grains are steamed and flattened to make rolled oats. In many countries, rolled oats are eaten as a breakfast porridge or mixed with fruit and seeds to make muesli or cereal.

2 Roughly chop the apricots and set them aside for later.

3 Put the butter, sugar and syrup in a pan and set it over a very low heat. Stir now and then, until the butter has melted.

4 When the butter has melted, remove the pan from the heat and stir the mixture well. Add the oats, seeds and apricots and stir again.

5 Tip the mixture into the tin and spread it out in an even layer. Make sure you push the mixture right into the corners of the tin.

6 Bake for about 25 minutes until golden. Wearing a pair of oven gloves, take the tin out of the oven and put it on a heatproof surface.

7 Leave the flapjack to cool in the tin. When cool, cut it into quarters. Then cut each quarter into four squares to make 16 squares in total.

Chocolate chip cookies

These simple biscuits, made with a creamed butter and sugar mixture, are a classic cookie. The soft mixture needs no shaping and can simply be dropped onto baking sheets in big dollops.

INGREDIENTS

For 20 cookies:
- 115g butter, at room temperature, plus extra for greasing
- 85g caster sugar • 1 egg, lightly beaten
- 1 tsp vanilla essence • 150g plain flour
- ½ tsp baking powder
- 100g chocolate chips

EXTRA EQUIPMENT
- 3 baking sheets • sieve
- wire rack

Ask an adult to help you use the oven.

1 Preheat the oven to 190°C/375°F/Gas 5. Grease the baking sheets with butter.

2 Put the butter and sugar in a bowl and beat them together with a wooden spoon until they make a smooth, creamy mixture.

3 Gradually add the egg to the butter mixture and beat well. Add the vanilla essence and beat the mixture until everything is mixed together.

4 Put the flour and baking powder in a clean bowl and mix them together. Sieve the flour into the butter mixture and stir until the mixture is creamy and well blended.

5 Add the chocolate chips and stir again.

6 Use a teaspoon to scoop up heaped spoonfuls of the mixture. Using another teaspoon, scrape the mixture onto the baking sheets. Space the blobs of cookie mixture well apart to allow them to spread during cooking. You should end up with about eight blobs of mixture on each baking sheet.

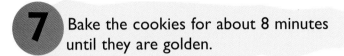

7 Bake the cookies for about 8 minutes until they are golden.

8 Using a pair of oven gloves, take the baking sheets out of the oven and put them on a heatproof surface. Leave the cookies to firm up for about 1 minute. When firm, lift the cookies onto a wire rack to cool.

MAKING CAKES AND BISCUITS RISE

Baking powder is a raising agent used to make cakes and biscuits rise. It is made from an alkali ingredient (bicarbonate of soda) and an acidic ingredient (cream of tartar). When these two ingredients come into contact with a wet ingredient, they react to make carbon dioxide. The carbon dioxide makes tiny bubbles in the cake or biscuit mixture, which cause it to rise.

Cheesy biscuits

These savoury biscuits are flavoured with tangy Cheddar cheese. When you want a treat, they make a great alternative to a traditional sweet biscuit.

INGREDIENTS
For 15 biscuits:
- 115g butter, at room temperature, plus extra for greasing
- 115g Cheddar cheese
- black pepper
- 150g self-raising flour • cold water

EXTRA EQUIPMENT
- 2 baking sheets • sieve
- wire rack

Ask an adult to help you use the oven.

1 Preheat the oven to 180°C/350°F/Gas 4. Grease two baking sheets with butter, making sure the surface is coated all over.

2 Grate the cheese.

3 Put the butter and cheese in a bowl and add a good grinding of black pepper. Beat them together until they make a soft, creamy mixture.

4 Sieve the flour into the butter mixture. Stir the mixture together and then bring it together with your hands.

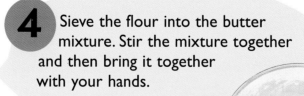

5 Break off walnut-sized lumps of mixture and roll them between your hands to make round balls. Place them on the baking sheets, spacing them well apart.

6 Dip a fork into cold water, then gently press onto the top of each ball to flatten it. You will need to keep dipping the fork in water to stop it sticking to the biscuit mixture.

7 Bake the biscuits for 15–20 minutes until they are golden brown.

8 Using a pair of oven gloves, take the baking sheets out of the oven and put them on a heatproof surface. Leave the biscuits to cool for a minute then use a metal spatula to lift them onto a wire rack to cool.

COOLING COOKIES

Most cookies need to be moved to a wire rack to cool soon after baking. This allows cool air to circulate all around the cookie, making sure it stays crisp. If the cookie was left on the baking sheet, condensation (or moisture) would make it soggy.

Victoria sandwich cake

This cake is made using a classic cake mixture. It uses equal weights of butter, sugar, eggs and flour. It is one of the easiest and most tasty sandwich cakes to make.

INGREDIENTS

For 1 sandwich cake:

- 175g butter, at room temperature, plus extra for greasing
- 175g caster sugar • 3 eggs
- 175g self-raising flour
- 4 tbsp strawberry jam • 1 tbsp icing sugar

EXTRA EQUIPMENT

- greaseproof paper • 2 20cm sandwich tins
- pencil • scissors • 2 wire racks

Ask an adult to help you use the oven

1 Preheat the oven to 180°C/350°F/Gas 4.

2 Cut off enough greaseproof paper to cover both sandwich tins. Place one of the tins on the edge of the paper and draw around it to make a circle. Repeat to make a second circle. Cut out the circles and check that they fit inside the tins. Set them aside.

3 Grease the inside of each tin with butter then slip a paper circle into the base of each tin and press it down flat.

4 Put the butter and sugar in a bowl and beat them until they are smooth and creamy. Break one egg into the mixture and beat the mixture well. Beat in another egg, then add the last egg and beat the mixture again.

5 Sieve the flour over the butter mixture then stir it gently until the mixture is creamy.

6 Spoon half of the mixture into one tin and spread it out with the back of the spoon. Spoon the remaining mixture into the second tin and spread it out.

HOW TO CRACK AN EGG

1. Hold the egg in one hand and knock the middle on the side of a bowl to make a deep crack in its shell.
2. Holding the egg over the bowl, put your thumbs into the crack.
3. Pull the halves apart so that the egg falls into the bowl. Check that no bits of shell fell into the bowl.

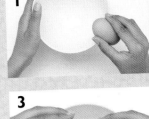

7 Bake for 20–25 minutes until each cake is golden and risen. To test if the cake is cooked, poke a skewer into the centre – it should come out clean. If the mixture sticks to the skewer then put the cake back into the oven for a few minutes more.

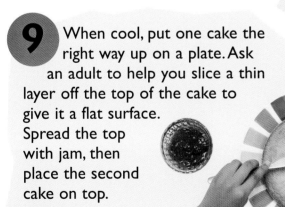

8 Use oven gloves to take the cakes out of the oven and put them on a heatproof surface. Ask an adult to help you to transfer the cakes to wire racks. Peel off the greaseproof paper and leave the cakes to cool.

9 When cool, put one cake the right way up on a plate. Ask an adult to help you slice a thin layer off the top of the cake to give it a flat surface. Spread the top with jam, then place the second cake on top.

10 Put the icing sugar in a sieve and hold it over the cake. Tap the side until the top of the cake is dusted with a layer of icing sugar.

Banana and fig muffins

Muffins are great for a weekend breakfast or brunch, or a teatime treat with a glass of milk. They are best eaten on the day you make them – that is why this recipe makes only six at a time.

INGREDIENTS

For 6 muffins:
- 50g butter • 125g self-raising flour
- ½ tsp baking powder
- ¼ tsp bicarbonate of soda
- 60g caster sugar
- 1 large ripe banana, peeled
- 1 egg • 50ml milk
- 4 ready-to-eat dried figs

EXTRA EQUIPMENT
- 6-hole muffin tray • 6 paper muffin cups
- sieve • wire rack

Ask an adult to help you use the oven.

1 Preheat the oven to 190°C/375°F/Gas 5. Put a paper muffin case inside each hole in the muffin tray.

2 Put the butter in a small pan and warm it over a gentle heat until it is melted. Set it aside.

3 Sieve the flour, baking powder, bicarbonate of soda and sugar into a bowl. Make a well in the middle of the ingredients.

4 Mash the banana. Add the egg, milk and melted butter to the banana and stir together until it is well mixed.

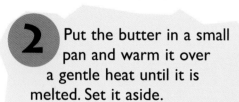

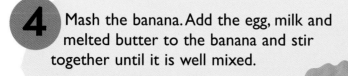

5 Cut the woody steams off the figs. Roughly chop the figs and add them to the banana mixture. Stir the mixture well.

DRIED FRUIT

Drying fruit preserves it and allows it to keep much longer than fresh fruit. Fruit can be dried by heat from the Sun or in a machine called a dehydrator. Drying fruit changes the texture and taste of the fruit, making it taste much stronger and sweeter.

6 Pour the banana mixture into the well in the dry ingredients. Mix all the ingredients together until they are just combined. Do not overmix them because the mixture needs to have a rough texture.

7 Using a tablespoon, spoon the muffin mixture into the paper cases. Bake for 20 minutes until the muffins are risen and golden.

8 Wearing a pair of oven gloves, carefully take the muffin tray out of the oven and put it on a heatproof surface. Using a clean tea towel to protect your hands, lift the muffins out of the tin and transfer them to a wire rack to cool. Serve warm or cold.

Candy cookies

These pretty cookies are fun to make and delicious to eat. You can be as creative as you like when it comes to decorating them. Spread a smooth layer of icing over each cookie and then decorate them with brightly coloured sweets.

INGREDIENTS

For 25–30 cookies:
- 175g butter, chilled, plus extra for greasing
- 225g plain flour, plus extra for dusting
- 125g caster sugar • 1 egg yolk

For the icing:
- 2 tbsp lemon juice
- 200g icing sugar, sifted
- small sweets to decorate

EXTRA EQUIPMENT
- food processor • clear film
- rolling pin • 6cm cookie cutter
- baking sheets • metal spatula

Ask an adult to help you use the oven.

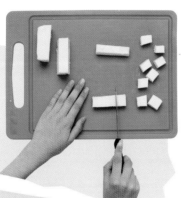

1 Cut the butter into dice.

2 Put the flour in a food processor and put the chilled butter on top of it. Turn on the food processor in short bursts until the mixture looks like fine breadcrumbs.

3 Add the egg yolk and sugar to the food processor and process until the mixture comes together in a ball.

4 Sprinkle a little flour onto your work surface then knead the dough until it is smooth. Shape it into a ball and wrap it in clear film. Put it in the fridge for at least 30 minutes to firm up.

SEPARATING EGGS

Some recipes call for just the yolk or just the white of an egg. To separate an egg, crack it against the edge of a bowl so that there is a deep crack in the shell. Put your fingers in the crack and pull the shell apart. Keep the yolk in one half of the shell and let the white fall into the bowl. Throw away the part of the egg that you do not need or keep it for another recipe.

5 Preheat the oven to 180°C/350°F/ Gas 4. Grease two baking sheets with butter.

6 Sprinkle a light layer of flour over your work surface, then put the ball of chilled dough on top and sprinkle it with a little more flour. Using a rolling pin, roll out the dough thinly.

7 Using the cookie cutter, cut out rounds from the dough, cutting as closely together as you can. Transfer the rounds to the baking sheets, spacing them slightly apart.

8 Bake the cookies for about 12 minutes until they are pale golden. Then use a pair of oven gloves to take the baking sheets out of the oven and put them on a heatproof surface. Slide a metal spatula underneath and lift the cookies onto the wire rack to cool.

9 To make the icing, put the lemon juice in a bowl and gradually stir in the icing sugar until it is smooth and looks like double cream.

10 Spread the icing onto the cookies and decorate them with coloured sweets.

Marshmallow fingers

This rich, squidgy cake is easy to make and requires no baking. Instead, you just need to chill it in the fridge.

1 Tear off a piece of clear film, wider and longer than the loaf tin and lay it on top of the tin. Press it down so that it covers the base of the tin. Let the extra clear film hang over the edges.

2 Put the nuts on a board and chop each one in half to use later.

3 Put the gingernuts in a plastic bag and twist the top of the bag to seal it. Hold the twisted top of the bag in one hand use a rolling pin to tap the biscuits to break them up into small pieces. Do not hit them too much or you will end up with just crumbs. If you have a few big bits of biscuit left in the bag, break these up with your fingers. Set the biscuits aside.

4 Pour water into a pan so that it is about 3cm deep. Rest a bowl inside the pan so it hangs above, but does not touch, the water. Put the pan over a medium heat and bring the water to the boil. Then turn the heat as low as it will go so that the water barely simmers.

5 Break the chocolate into pieces and put it in the bowl with the butter. Wait until it is nearly melted, then remove it from the heat and leave it to stand for a few minutes. Stir the chocolate until both the chocolate and butter are completely melted.

SOLID CHOCOLATE

Chocolate is a solid but it can be melted and changed into a liquid. When the runny chocolate is cooled, it hardens to become a solid again. This type of change is called a reversible change because it can continue to happen.

6 Add the nuts, biscuits and marshmallows to the chocolate and stir until they are well mixed.

7 Tip the mixture into the tin and spread it out in an even layer, pressing down with a spoon. Fold the overhanging clear film over the top so the mixture is covered. Press down on the covered mixture to make sure it is firmly packed in the tin.

8 Put the tin in the fridge for 2 hours until it is firm. Then tip the tin upside down so that the cake falls out. Unwrap the cake and place it on a chopping board.

9 Cut the cake into fingers. Dust the fingers with icing sugar to serve.

19

Vanilla cupcakes

Cupcakes topped with creamy icing are easy to make. You can choose whatever colour you like for the icing – yellow, pink, lilac, green or blue will all look great.

INGREDIENTS

For 12 cupcakes:
- 115g butter, at room temperature
- 115g caster sugar • 2 eggs
- ½ tsp vanilla essence
- 115g self-raising flour

For the icing:
- 75g butter • 225g icing sugar
- 2 tbsp milk • ¼ tsp vanilla essence
- food colouring • hundreds and thousands

EXTRA EQUIPMENT

- 12-hole cupcake tray
- 12 paper cupcake cases • sieve
- wire rack

Ask an adult to help you use the oven.

1 Preheat the oven to 180°C/350°F/Gas 4. Put a paper cupcake case inside each hole in the cupcake tray.

2 Put the butter and caster sugar in a bowl and beat them to make a pale, creamy mixture.

3 Lightly beat the eggs and add them and the vanilla to the butter mixture a little at a time. Beat until the mixture is smooth.

4 Sieve the flour into the butter mixture and stir until it makes a smooth, creamy mixture.

5 Drop spoonfuls of the mixture into the cupcake cases until you have divided the mixture evenly between the cases.

6 Bake the cupcakes for 18 minutes until they are risen and golden. Wearing a pair of oven gloves, remove the tray from the oven and place it on a heatproof surface. After about a minute, transfer the cakes to a wire rack to cool.

7 When the cakes are cool, they are ready to decorate. Put the butter in a medium bowl and beat until it is creamy. Sieve the icing sugar over the butter and add the milk and vanilla. Stir together until creamy. Add 1 or 2 drops of food colouring and stir well to mix.

8 Spread the icing on top of the cakes, then sprinkle over hundreds and thousands.

TESTING IF THEY ARE COOKED

To check if your cupcakes are cooked, gently press the top of a cake with the tip of your finger. If it is cooked, the top will spring back. If it does not spring back, the cakes need to go back in the oven for another minute or two.

Glossary

acid

A substance that contains the gas hydrogen and causes chemical change. Cream of tartar is an acid.

alkali

A substance that neutralises (balances out) acids. Bicarbonate of soda is an alkali.

carbon dioxide

A colourless gas. Baking powder and self-raising flour produce tiny bubbles of carbon dioxide, which make cake and cookie mixtures rise in the oven.

circulate

To move around and come back to the beginning.

coarse

When something is rough.

glacé fruit

When fruit is preserved or stored in sugar so that it has a glossy or shiny look.

glacé icing

Icing made from icing sugar and water.

kneading

To press and stretch dough until it is soft and stretchy.

liquid

A substance, such as water, that can flow but is not a gas.

muesli

A breakfast food made from cereal, nuts and dried fruit.

reversible change

A chemical change that can keep happening.

savoury

When flavours are tasty but not sweet. For example, cheese has a savoury flavour.

solid

A substance, such as wood, that keeps its shape.

texture

The way the surface of something feels.

well

A hollow or dip made in the middle of a mixture of flour into which liquid is poured.

EXTRA INFORMATION

These abbreviations have been used:
• tbsp – tablespoon • tsp – teaspoon
• ml – millilitre • g – gram • l – litre

To work out where the cooker dial needs to be for high, medium and low heat, count the marks on the dial and divide it by three. The top few are high and the bottom few are low. The in-between ones are medium.

All eggs are medium unless stated

Equipment

PLASTIC SPATULA

These are great for scraping mixtures from the sides of bowls.

ROLLING PIN
Round wooden rolling pins can be used to roll out cookie dough.

MEASURING SPOONS
Measuring spoons help you to use the exact amount of ingredients.

CUTTERS

These come in many different shapes and sizes. Use them to cut out rolled dough.

MEASURING CUPS

These are used just like measuring spoons but for measuring bigger quantities of ingredients.

GREASEPROOF PAPER
Use to line baking trays and cake tins to prevent mixtures sticking to the surface.

BAKING SHEETS

Metal sheets for baking food in the oven.

BUN TRAYS

These come in different sizes and are good for baking cupcakes and muffins.

SIEVE

These may be small, medium or large and are useful for sifting flour and icing sugar.

WIRE RACK
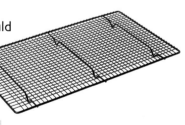
Cakes and biscuits should always be cooled on a wire rack to allow air to circulate underneath.

BAKING TINS

These come in all shapes and sizes so you can bake different shaped cakes.

SCALES
Use to measure dry and solid ingredients accurately.

Index